PRINCIPLES FOR MAKING MARRIAGE WORK

UNDERSTAND WHAT WORKS FOR LASTING MARRIAGE

Table of Content

Book Description

You would learn the following from this book

1. **You would learn how to navigate complexity in your marriage**
2. **Principle that foster strong and lasting relationship**
3. **Dynamics Within relationship and to cultivate deeper connections with your partner**
4. **Emphasis on communication , emotional intelligence and understanding the dynamics of conflict**
5. **Importance of fostering positive interactions and building a foundation of trust and respect**

INTRODUCTION

Navigating complexity in marriage requires a deep understanding of each other's experiences and emotions. Clinical experience and emotional intelligence play a crucial role in building deeper connections and effective communication within the relationship.

Clinical experience can provide valuable insights into understanding the complexities of human behavior and emotions. It can help individuals navigate through challenges and conflicts within the marriage, and provide tools and techniques to improve communication and emotional connection.

Furthermore, emotional intelligence plays a vital role in understanding and managing one's own emotions, as well as understanding and empathizing with the emotions of their partner. It involves being aware of one's own feelings and the feelings of others, and using this awareness to navigate through complex situations in a marriage.

Effective communication is also essential in navigating complexity in marriage. It involves actively listening to each other, expressing thoughts and emotions openly and honestly, and finding common ground to resolve conflicts and challenges.

We shall be diving into the real matter on navigating complexity, clinical experience, emotional intelligence effective communication and lot more of it .

CHAPTER 1

NATIVIGATING COMPLEXITY IN MARRIAGE

Navigating complexity in marriage can be challenging but there is rewarding process. It involves understanding and addressing the various layers of emotions, communication styles, and life circumstances that can impact a relationship.

Here are some key aspects to consider when navigating complexity in marriage:

1. Effective Communication: Open, honest, and respectful communication is essential in navigating complexity in marriage. It's important for both partners to actively listen to each other, express their thoughts and feelings, and work towards finding common ground.

2. Emotional Intelligence: Developing emotional intelligence can help partners understand and manage their own emotions, as well as empathize with their spouse's feelings. This can lead to more empathy, compassion, and understanding within the relationship.

3. Clinical Experience: Seeking guidance from a therapist or counselor with clinical experience can provide valuable insights and tools for navigating through complex issues in the marriage. Professional support can help couples work through challenges and develop healthier ways of relating to each other.

4. Building Deeper Connections: Nurturing a deeper connection in marriage involves being present for each other, showing empathy, and creating a safe space for vulnerability and trust. This can help partners navigate through the complexities of life together.

5. Resilience and Adaptability: Marriage often requires flexibility and resilience to navigate through life's ups and downs. Being adaptable and willing to grow and change together can help couples navigate complexity in their relationship.

Ultimately, navigating complexity in marriage requires a commitment from both partners to work through challenges, communicate effectively, and continuously nurture their connection. It's an ongoing journey that can lead to a deeper and more fulfilling relationship.

CHAPTER 2

PRINCIPLE THAT FOASTER STRONG AND LASTING RELATIONSHIPS

The principle that fosters strong and lasting relationships is based on several key elements.

These include: Communication: Open, honest, and respectful communication is essential in any relationship. This involves active listening, expressing thoughts and feelings, and working through challenges together.

1. Trust and Respect: Trust and respect form the foundation of a strong relationship. Building trust through honesty, reliability, and mutual respect is crucial for a lasting bond.

2. Empathy and Understanding: Being able to understand and empathize with your partner's feelings and experiences helps create a deeper connection and fosters a sense of closeness.

3. Commitment: Both partners need to be committed to the relationship and willing to invest time, effort, and resources into nurturing and maintaining it.

4. Compromise and Flexibility: Relationships require compromise and flexibility. Being open to each other's needs and finding solutions that work for both parties is crucial for long-term success.

5. Shared Values and Goals: Having shared values and working towards common goals can create a sense of unity and purpose within the relationship.

6. Emotional Support: Providing emotional support and being there for each other during challenging times is essential for a strong and lasting bond.

By incorporating these principles into a relationship, couples can build a solid foundation that fosters a strong and lasting connection.

CHAPTER 3

CLINICAL EXPERIENCE TO OUTLINE ACTIONABLE STRATEGIES IN MARRIAGE

Clinical experience can provide valuable insights and actionable strategies to help couples navigate challenges and strengthen the marriage.

Here are some actionable strategies that can be outlined through clinical experience:

Communication Skills Training: Clinical experience can offer specific communication techniques and strategies to improve dialogue between partners. This may include active listening, assertive expression of feelings, and conflict resolution skills.

1. Emotion Regulation Techniques: Clinical professionals can provide tools and techniques to help individuals regulate and manage their emotions, which can be crucial in maintaining healthy interactions within the marriage.

2. Couples Counseling: Clinical experience can involve couples counseling, where both partners can work with a therapist to address specific issues, improve their understanding of each other, and develop strategies to enhance their relationship.

3. Cognitive Behavioral Therapy (CBT): CBT techniques can be applied to help individuals identify and change negative thought patterns and behaviors that may be impacting

their marriage. This can lead to more positive interactions and a healthier relationship dynamic.

4. Stress Management and Coping Strategies: Clinical professionals can offer stress management techniques and coping strategies to help couples navigate the challenges of daily life, reducing the impact of stress on the relationship.
5. Conflict Resolution Skills: Clinical experience can provide structured approaches to resolving conflicts within the marriage, compromising , understanding, and mutual respect.
6. Building Intimacy and Connection: Clinical professionals can guide couples in developing strategies to enhance intimacy and connection, including techniques for emotional and physical closeness.

By utilizing actionable strategies outlined through clinical experience, couples can work towards building a healthier, more fulfilling marriage. These strategies can help address specific challenges, improve communication, and foster a stronger bond between partners.

CHAPTER 4

HOW TO CULTIVATE DEEPER CONNECTIONS WITH PARTNER IN MARRIAGE

Cultivating deeper connections with your partner in marriage involves intentional effort and commitment. Here are some strategies to help foster a deeper connection:

1. Quality Time: Spend quality time together regularly, engaging in activities that you both enjoy. This could be anything from going for a walk, cooking together, or simply having a meaningful conversation.

2. Effective Communication: Practice open and honest communication. Share your thoughts, feelings, and experiences with each other, and actively listen to your partner without judgment.

3. Emotional Support: Be there for your partner during both the good and challenging times. Offering emotional support and understanding can strengthen your bond.

4. Shared Experiences: Create and share experiences together. This could involve traveling, pursuing a hobby together, or setting and achieving shared goals.

5. Physical Affection: Physical touch and affection play a significant role in building a deeper connection. Simple gestures like holding hands, hugging, and physical intimacy can strengthen your bond.

6. Express Gratitude: Regularly express appreciation and gratitude for your partner. Recognizing and acknowledging their positive qualities and contributions to the relationship can deepen your connection.

7. Vulnerability and Trust: Cultivate an environment of trust and vulnerability where both partners feel safe to share their true selves without fear of judgment.

8. Shared Values and Goals: Identify and work towards shared values and goals. Having a common purpose can create a sense of unity and deepen your connection.

Seek Couples Counseling: If needed, consider seeking couples counseling. A professional therapist can provide guidance and tools to help you and your partner understand each other better and strengthen your bond.

By incorporating these strategies into your marriage, you can cultivate a deeper and more meaningful connection with your partner. It's important to remember that building a deeper connection is an ongoing process that requires effort and nurturing from both partners.

CHAPTER 5

EMPHASIS ON COMMUNICATION, EMOTIONAL INTELLIGENCE

Emphasizing communication and emotional intelligence can significantly contribute to cultivating a deeper connection with your partner in marriage. Here's how to focus on these aspects:

1. Active Listening: Practice active listening, which involves fully concentrating, understanding, responding, and remembering what your partner is saying. This demonstrates respect and empathy, and it encourages open communication.

2. Expressing Emotions: Encourage open expression of emotions. Create a safe space where both partners feel comfortable sharing their feelings without fear of judgment or dismissal.

3. Emotional Awareness: Develop emotional intelligence by becoming more aware of your own emotions and understanding how they impact your thoughts and behavior. This self-awareness can help you communicate more effectively with your partner.

4. Empathy: Cultivate empathy by seeking to understand your partner's perspective and emotions. This can help you respond to your partner's needs and concerns in a more supportive and compassionate manner.

5. Non-Verbal Communication: Pay attention to non-verbal cues, such as body language and facial expressions, as they can convey emotions and feelings that may not be expressed verbally.

6. Conflict Resolution: Develop effective conflict resolution skills by approaching disagreements with a focus on understanding and compromise rather than winning or being right. This can foster a more harmonious and respectful communication style.

7. Mindful Communication: Practice mindful communication by being present and attentive during conversations with your partner. This can help you better understand their emotions and respond thoughtfully.

8. Seek Feedback: Encourage open feedback from your partner about your communication style and emotional responsiveness. This can help you identify areas for improvement and strengthen your connection.

By placing a strong emphasis on communication and emotional intelligence within your marriage, you can create an environment where both partners feel heard, understood, and supported, leading to a deeper and more fulfilling connection.

CHAPTER 6

UNDERSTANDING DYNAMICS OF CONFLICT

Understanding the dynamics of conflict within a marriage is crucial for navigating disagreements in a healthy and constructive manner. Here are some key aspects to consider:

1. Triggers: Identify the triggers that lead to conflicts. These triggers can be related to specific behaviors, communication patterns, or unmet emotional needs. Understanding these triggers can help prevent conflicts from escalating.

2. Communication Styles: Recognize how you and your partner communicate during conflicts. Understanding each other's communication styles, such as passive, aggressive, or assertive, can help in finding common ground and resolving conflicts more effectively.

3. Emotional Responses: Be aware of your own and your partner's emotional responses during conflicts. Understanding the underlying emotions, such as anger, fear, or hurt, can help address the root causes of the conflict.

4. Power Dynamics: Recognize any power imbalances or control issues that may influence the dynamics of conflicts. Addressing these dynamics can help create a more equitable and respectful environment for conflict resolution.

5. Listening and Validation: Practice active listening and validate your partner's feelings during conflicts. Feeling heard and understood can de-escalate conflicts and promote mutual understanding.

6. Compromise and Collaboration: Understand the importance of compromise and collaboration in resolving conflicts. Focus on finding solutions that meet both partners' needs and promote the well-being of the relationship.

7. Timing and Environment: Consider the timing and environment in which conflicts are addressed. Choosing the right time and creating a safe and calm space for discussions can contribute to more productive conflict resolution.

8.Seeking Professional Help: If conflicts become persistent or unmanageable, consider seeking the guidance of a couples therapist. A professional can help you understand the underlying dynamics of conflicts and provide tools for effective resolution.

By understanding the dynamics of conflict within your marriage, you can approach disagreements with greater awareness,

empathy, and a focus on finding constructive solutions that strengthen your relationship.

CHAPTER 6

IMPORTANCE OF FOSTERING POSITIVE INTERACTIONS AND BUILDING FOUNDATION ON TRUST

Fostering positive interactions and building a foundation of trust are fundamental for creating a healthy and resilient marriage. Here's why these aspects are crucial:

1. Emotional Connection: Positive interactions, such as shared laughter, affectionate gestures, and quality time together, contribute to building a strong emotional connection between partners. These interactions create a sense of closeness and intimacy that strengthens the bond.

2. Resilience During Challenges: Building a foundation of trust through positive interactions creates a sense of

3. security and support within the relationship. This foundation of trust can help couples navigate challenges and conflicts with greater resilience and unity.

4. Communication: Positive interactions contribute to open and effective communication. When couples engage in positive interactions, they are more likely to communicate openly, express appreciation, and address concerns in a constructive manner.

5. Shared Joy and Fulfillment: Positive interactions foster an environment where both partners can experience joy, fulfillment, and a sense of mutual support. This can lead to a more satisfying and rewarding marriage.

6. Conflict Resolution: Positive interactions build a reservoir of goodwill and positive experiences that can be drawn upon during conflicts. They can serve as a reminder of the love and respect within the relationship, making it easier to resolve conflicts.

7. Trust and Security: Building a foundation of trust through positive interactions creates a sense of security within the relationship. Trust allows partners to be vulnerable, express themselves authentically, and rely on each other for emotional support.

8. Long-Term Satisfaction: Research has shown that marriages characterized by positive interactions and trust tend to have higher levels of long-term satisfaction and lower rates of divorce By prioritizing positive interactions and building a foundation of trust, couples can create a nurturing and supportive environment that strengthens

their bond and paves the way for a fulfilling and enduring marriage.

31

CONCLUSION

In conclusion, navigating complexity in marriage requires clinical experience, emotional intelligence, effective communication, and a commitment to building deeper connections. By embracing these qualities, couples can navigate through challenges and conflicts, and build a strong and resilient relationship.